C# and NET

MODERN CROSS-PLATFORM DEVELOPMENT

OLIVER LUCAS JR

Preface

Welcome to the world of cross-platform development with C# and .NET 6! This book is your guide to building modern, high-performance applications that run seamlessly on Windows, macOS, Linux, iOS, Android, and more.

.NET has undergone a remarkable transformation in recent years, evolving from a Windows-centric framework to a powerful, open-source, and cross-platform powerhouse. .NET 6, with its unified platform and focus on performance, represents a significant leap forward, empowering developers to create applications that can reach users on any device, anywhere in the world.

This book is designed for developers of all levels, from those just starting their journey with C# to experienced programmers looking to expand their skills into the realm of cross-platform development. Whether you're building mobile apps, desktop applications, games, or cloud services, this book provides the knowledge and tools you need to succeed.

What you'll learn:

The evolution of .NET: Understand the journey from .NET Framework to .NET 6 and the rise of cross-platform development.

C# fundamentals: Master the core language features of C#, including data types, operators, control flow, and object-oriented programming.

Building user interfaces: Create stunning cross-platform UIs with .NET MAUI, leveraging its powerful controls and layout capabilities.

Accessing data and services: Connect to databases, consume RESTful APIs, and integrate with cloud services like Azure.

Developing mobile and desktop applications: Build native mobile apps for iOS and Android, and create desktop applications for Windows, macOS, and Linux.

Testing and debugging: Implement unit testing and debugging techniques to ensure the quality and reliability of your code.

Advanced topics: Explore advanced concepts like asynchronous programming, multithreading, security, and internationalization.

Game development: Discover the possibilities of game development with .NET and popular game engines.

Future trends: Stay ahead of the curve with insights into emerging trends and technologies in the .NET ecosystem.

Why this book is different:

Focus on .NET 6 and .NET MAUI: This book is specifically tailored to the latest advancements in .NET, with a strong emphasis on .NET MAUI for cross-platform UI development.

Practical approach: Learn through hands-on examples, code snippets, and real-world scenarios.

Comprehensive coverage: Explore a wide range of topics, from basic concepts to advanced techniques, providing a holistic view of cross-platform development with C#.

Clear and concise writing: Complex concepts are explained in a clear and accessible manner, making it easy to grasp even for beginners.

TABLE OF CONTENTS

Chapter 1

Introduction to Cross-Platform Development with C# and .NET 6

1.1 The Early Days: .NET Framework and Windows Dominance

In the early 2000s, Microsoft introduced the .NET Framework, a revolutionary platform designed to simplify Windows application development. It brought with it a host of powerful features, ushering in a new era of software development:

Managed Code: Instead of wrestling with the complexities of manual memory management, developers could rely on the .NET Framework's garbage collector to automatically handle memory allocation and deallocation. This simplified development and reduced the risk of memory leaks, making applications more robust and reliable.

Common Language Runtime (CLR): This virtual machine acted as the foundation of the .NET Framework, providing a consistent execution environment for different programming languages. This meant that developers could write code in C#, Visual Basic .NET, or other languages that targeted the .NET Framework, and the CLR would ensure that it ran correctly on any Windows machine.

Rich Class Library: The .NET Framework included a vast collection of pre-built components and libraries, offering ready-made solutions for common programming tasks. This significantly accelerated development, allowing developers to focus on building their applications' unique features rather than reinventing the wheel.

The .NET Framework quickly gained popularity, becoming the go-to platform for Windows developers. It enabled the creation of countless successful applications, including:

Desktop Applications: Microsoft Office, Visual Studio, and numerous other productivity tools relied on the .NET Framework for their rich functionality and user-friendly interfaces.

Web Applications: ASP.NET, a powerful web development framework built on the .NET Framework, powered businesses of all sizes, enabling dynamic websites and interactive web services.

Games: The XNA framework, built on top of the .NET Framework, allowed developers to create engaging games for Windows and the Xbox 360, showcasing the platform's versatility.

However, as technology advanced and the computing landscape shifted towards mobile devices and cloud services, the limitations of the .NET Framework became apparent. Its tight coupling with Windows hindered its adoption on other platforms, and its monolithic architecture presented challenges for deployment and maintenance in the rapidly evolving world of software development.

1.2 Why Choose C# and .NET 6 for Your Next Project?

In today's crowded landscape of programming languages and frameworks, choosing the right tools for your project can be a daunting task. C# and .NET 6 emerge as a compelling combination, offering a unique blend of power, versatility, and modern features that make them an excellent choice for a wide range of applications. Here's why:

Cross-Platform Powerhouse: .NET 6 truly breaks down platform barriers. Whether you're targeting Windows, macOS, Linux, iOS, Android, or even embedded systems, .NET 6 provides a consistent and reliable foundation for your development efforts. This cross-platform capability allows you to reach a wider audience and maximize the impact of your applications.

Blazing Performance: .NET 6 is renowned for its exceptional performance. Thanks to continuous optimizations in the runtime and libraries, .NET 6 applications run faster and consume fewer resources, leading to improved user experiences and reduced infrastructure costs.

Developer Productivity: C# is a modern, elegant language designed for developer productivity. Its clear syntax, powerful features like LINQ (Language Integrated Query), and extensive libraries make it easier to write clean, maintainable code. The .NET ecosystem also provides excellent tooling support with Visual Studio and Visual Studio Code, further enhancing developer efficiency.

Thriving Ecosystem: The .NET community is vast and active, offering a wealth of resources, libraries, and support. This vibrant ecosystem ensures that you're never alone on your development journey. Whether you need help with a specific problem, want to explore new libraries, or simply want to connect with fellow developers, the .NET community has you covered.

Future-Proof Foundation: .NET is actively developed and maintained by Microsoft, with a clear roadmap for future enhancements and innovations. This ensures that your investment in .NET 6 will continue to pay dividends in the years to come, as the platform evolves to meet the demands of the ever-changing technological landscape.

Versatility: From web applications and mobile apps to desktop software, games, and cloud services, C# and .NET 6 can handle it all. This versatility makes it a strategic choice for organizations and developers who want to build a diverse range of applications with a single, unified technology stack.

By choosing C# and .NET 6, you're not just choosing a technology; you're investing in a powerful, versatile, and future-proof platform that empowers you to bring your ideas to life and build applications that truly matter.

1.3 Setting Up Your Development Environment for Cross-Platform Success

Before you embark on your cross-platform development journey with C# and .NET 6, it's essential to set up a robust and efficient development environment. This will ensure a smooth workflow and allow you to build, test, and debug your applications seamlessly across different operating systems. Here's a step-by-step guide to get you started:

1. Install the .NET 6 SDK:

Head over to the official .NET website (https://dotnet.microsoft.com/download) and download the .NET 6 SDK for your operating system (Windows, macOS, or Linux).

Run the installer and follow the on-screen instructions. This will install the necessary tools, including the C# compiler, the .NET CLI, and the .NET runtime.

2. Choose Your IDE (Integrated Development Environment):

Visual Studio: If you're on Windows, Visual Studio is the recommended IDE for .NET development. It offers a comprehensive set of features, including a powerful debugger, intelligent code completion, and integrated testing tools. Download the Community edition for free or choose a more feature-rich edition like Professional or Enterprise.

Visual Studio Code: A lightweight and versatile code editor that works across all major operating systems. With the C# extension, Visual Studio Code becomes a powerful .NET development environment. It's a great choice if you prefer a more minimalist approach or are working on a machine with limited resources.

JetBrains Rider: A cross-platform IDE from JetBrains that provides excellent support for .NET development. It offers a similar feature set to Visual Studio, with a focus on code quality and developer productivity.

3. Install Platform-Specific SDKs (If Needed):

If you're planning to develop mobile applications for iOS or Android, you'll need to install the respective platform SDKs:

iOS: Xcode from the Mac App Store.

Android: Android Studio from the Android developer website.

For other platforms, such as macOS or Linux, the .NET 6 SDK provides the necessary tools to build and run applications.

4. Configure Your IDE:

Once you've installed your chosen IDE, take some time to configure it for .NET development. This may involve:

Installing necessary extensions (e.g., the C# extension for Visual Studio Code).

Configuring build settings and debugging options.

Customizing the editor to match your preferences.

5. Explore the .NET CLI:

The .NET CLI (Command Line Interface) is a powerful tool for managing .NET projects and performing various development tasks. Familiarize yourself with its commands for creating, building, running, and publishing applications.

6. Set Up Version Control:

Use a version control system like Git to track your code changes and collaborate with others. This is essential for any software development project, especially when working in a cross-platform environment.

7. Start Building!

With your development environment set up, you're ready to start building cross-platform applications with C# and .NET 6. Explore the different project templates available in your IDE or the .NET CLI to get started.

By following these steps, you'll create a solid foundation for your cross-platform development journey. Remember to keep your tools updated and explore the vast resources available in the .NET ecosystem to continuously enhance your development skills.

Chapter 2

C# Fundamentals for Cross-Platform Development

2.1 Core Language Features: Data Types, Operators, and Control Flow

C# provides a rich set of core language features that form the building blocks of any application. Understanding these fundamentals is crucial for writing effective and efficient code. Let's explore the essential concepts of data types, operators, and control flow.

Data Types:

In C#, data types define the kind of values a variable can hold and the operations that can be performed on it. Here are some commonly used data types:

Numeric Types:

`int`: For storing whole numbers (integers) like 10, -5, or 1000.

`double`: For storing floating-point numbers (numbers with decimal points) like 3.14, -2.5, or 0.001.

`decimal`: For high-precision decimal numbers, often used in financial applications.

Textual Type:

`string`: For storing sequences of characters like "Hello, world!" or "C# is awesome!".

Boolean Type:

`bool`: Represents a logical value, either `true` or `false`.

Character Type:

`char`: Represents a single character, like 'A', '?', or '$'.

Operators:

Operators are symbols that perform operations on data. C# provides a variety of operators, including:

Arithmetic Operators: `+`, `-`, `*`, `/`, `%` (modulo) for performing mathematical calculations.

Comparison Operators: `==` (equals), `!=` (not equals), `>`, `<`, `>=`, `<=` for comparing values.

Logical Operators: `&&` (and), `||` (or), `!` (not) for combining logical conditions.

Assignment Operator: `=` for assigning values to variables.

Control Flow Statements:

Control flow statements determine the order in which code is executed. C# provides several control flow statements, including:

Conditional Statements:

`if-else`: Executes different blocks of code based on a condition.

`switch`: Selects a block of code to execute based on the value of an expression.

Looping Statements:

`for`: Repeats a block of code a specific number of times.

`while`: Repeats a block of code as long as a condition is true.

`do-while`: Similar to `while`, but the code block is executed at least once.

Example:

Code snippet

```
int age = 25;
if (age >= 18)
{
    Console.WriteLine("You are an adult.");
}
else
{
    Console.WriteLine("You are a minor.");
}
```

In this example, the `if-else` statement checks if the `age` variable is greater than or equal to 18. If it is, the first block of code is executed; otherwise, the second block is executed.

Understanding these core language features is essential for writing any C# program. As you progress through this book, you'll see how these concepts are applied in various scenarios to build powerful and versatile applications.

2.2 Object-Oriented Programming in C#: Classes, Inheritance, and Polymorphism

Object-oriented programming (OOP) is a powerful paradigm that allows you to structure your code around objects, which combine data and behavior. C# is a fully object-oriented language, providing robust support for key OOP concepts like classes, inheritance, and polymorphism.

Classes:

A class is a blueprint for creating objects. It defines a set of properties (data) and methods (behavior) that the objects of that class will have. Think of a class as a template or a cookie cutter – it defines the structure and capabilities, but you need to create objects (the cookies) from it to actually use it.

Code snippet

```
public class Dog
{
    // Properties
    public string Name { get; set; }
    public string Breed { get; set; }

    // Method
    public void Bark()
    {
        Console.WriteLine("Woof!");
    }
}
```

In this example, `Dog` is a class with properties `Name` and `Breed` and a method `Bark()`.

Inheritance:

Inheritance allows you to create new classes (derived classes) that inherit properties and methods from existing classes (base classes). This promotes code reuse and allows you to create hierarchies of classes with specialized functionalities.

Code snippet

```
public class Poodle : Dog
{
    public void Prance()
    {
            Console.WriteLine("The poodle prances
around.");
    }
}
```

Here, `Poodle` inherits from `Dog`, so it automatically has `Name`, `Breed`, and `Bark()`. It also adds its own specialized method, `Prance()`.

Polymorphism:

Polymorphism (meaning "many forms") allows objects of different classes to be treated as objects of a common type. This enables you to write more flexible and maintainable code.

Code snippet

```
Dog myDog = new Dog();
myDog.Bark(); // Outputs "Woof!"

Dog myPoodle = new Poodle();
myPoodle.Bark();  //  Outputs  "Woof!"  (inherited
from Dog)
```

Even though `myPoodle` is a `Poodle` object, it can be treated as a `Dog` object. This is polymorphism in action.

Key Benefits of OOP:

Code Reusability: Inheritance allows you to reuse code from existing classes, reducing redundancy.

Modularity: Classes encapsulate data and behavior, making code more organized and easier to maintain.

Flexibility: Polymorphism allows you to write code that can work with objects of different classes, making your applications more adaptable to change.

Maintainability: OOP promotes clean code structure, making it easier to understand, debug, and modify.

By mastering these OOP principles, you'll be able to write more efficient, robust, and scalable C# applications.

2.3 Working with Data: Collections, LINQ, and File I/O

Data is the lifeblood of any application. C# provides powerful tools for working with data, including collections for storing and organizing data in memory, LINQ for querying and manipulating data, and file I/O for reading and writing data to files.

Collections:

Collections are classes that allow you to store and manage groups of objects. C# offers a variety of collection types, each with its own characteristics and use cases:

Lists (`List<T>`): Ordered collections that can grow or shrink dynamically. You can access elements by their index.

Code snippet

```
List<string>   names   =   new   List<string>()   {
"Alice", "Bob", "Charlie" };
names.Add("David");
Console.WriteLine(names[0]); // Outputs "Alice"
```

Arrays (`T[]`**):** Fixed-size collections that store elements of the same type. Efficient for accessing elements by index.

Code snippet

```
int[] numbers = new int[5] { 1, 2, 3, 4, 5 };
numbers[2] = 10;
Console.WriteLine(numbers[2]); // Outputs 10
```

Dictionaries (`Dictionary<TKey, TValue>`**):** Store key-value pairs, allowing you to access values efficiently by their keys.

Code snippet

```
Dictionary<string,     int>     ages     =     new
Dictionary<string, int>();
ages.Add("Alice", 30);
Console.WriteLine(ages["Alice"]); // Outputs 30
```

LINQ (Language Integrated Query):

LINQ provides a consistent and expressive way to query and manipulate data from various sources, including collections, databases, and XML documents. It allows you to write queries using familiar C# syntax.

Code snippet

```
List<int> numbers = new List<int>() { 1, 2, 3, 4,
5 };

// Using LINQ to find even numbers
var evenNumbers = from num in numbers
                  where num % 2 == 0
                  select num;

foreach (var number in evenNumbers)
{
    Console.WriteLine(number);[1] // Outputs 2 and
4
}
```

File I/O:

C# provides classes for reading from and writing to files. This allows you to persist data, import data from external sources, and export data for use in other applications.

Code snippet

```
// Writing to a file
string text = "This is some text.";
File.WriteAllText("myfile.txt", text);
```

```
// Reading from a file
string content = File.ReadAllText("myfile.txt");
Console.WriteLine(content); // Outputs "This is
some text."
```

By combining collections, LINQ, and file I/O, you can effectively manage and process data in your C# applications, whether it's stored in memory, a database, or a file.

Chapter 3

Building Cross-Platform User Interfaces with .NET MAUI

You're diving into the heart of cross-platform UI development with .NET MAUI! Here's a draft for "Introduction to .NET MAUI: A Unified Framework for UI Development":

3.1 Introduction to .NET MAUI: A Unified Framework for UI Development

.NET MAUI (Multi-platform App UI) is a revolutionary framework that transforms the way you build native user interfaces for mobile and desktop applications. It allows you to create stunning, performant UIs with a single codebase that runs seamlessly on Android, iOS, macOS, and Windows.

What makes .NET MAUI so special?

Single Codebase, Multiple Platforms: Write your UI code once in C# and XAML and deploy it across all supported platforms. This dramatically reduces development time and effort, allowing you to reach a wider audience with less code.

Native Performance: .NET MAUI leverages platform-specific UI controls, ensuring that your applications look and feel native on each operating system. This provides a superior user experience compared to traditional cross-platform solutions that rely on web-based rendering.

Modern Architecture: .NET MAUI is built on top of .NET 6, taking advantage of its performance improvements and modern features. This ensures that your applications are built on a solid and future-proof foundation.

Rich UI Controls: .NET MAUI provides a comprehensive set of UI controls, from basic elements like buttons and labels to more complex controls like lists, grids, and navigation elements. These controls are designed to be flexible and customizable, allowing you to create unique and engaging user interfaces.

Extensible and Customizable: .NET MAUI is highly extensible, allowing you to create custom controls, integrate with third-party libraries, and access platform-specific APIs. This gives you the freedom to tailor your applications to meet specific requirements.

How does .NET MAUI work?

.NET MAUI acts as a bridge between your C# code and the native UI frameworks of each platform. When you compile your .NET MAUI application, it generates native code that uses the platform's UI controls, resulting in a truly native look and feel.

Key components of .NET MAUI:

XAML: A declarative markup language for defining user interfaces. XAML allows you to describe the structure and appearance of your UI in a human-readable format.

C#: The programming language used to handle the logic and behavior of your application. C# interacts with the UI defined in XAML to create dynamic and interactive experiences.

.NET MAUI Essentials: A library that provides access to common device features like sensors, geolocation, and secure storage. This allows you to create applications that interact with the user's device in meaningful ways.

.NET MAUI represents a significant leap forward in cross-platform UI development. It empowers developers to create beautiful, native applications with unprecedented efficiency and reach.

3.2 Building Your First .NET MAUI Application: A Cross-Platform Hello World

It's time to put .NET MAUI into action and build your first cross-platform application! We'll create a simple "Hello, World!" app that runs on Android, iOS, macOS, and Windows. This will give you a taste of .NET MAUI's power and simplicity.

Prerequisites:

You have set up your .NET MAUI development environment as described in Chapter 1.

You have a basic understanding of C# and XAML (refer to Chapter 2 if needed).

Let's get started!

Create a new .NET MAUI project:

Open Visual Studio and select "Create a new project."

Search for the ".NET MAUI App" template and click "Next."

Give your project a name (e.g., "MyFirstMauiApp") and choose a location to save it.

Click "Create" to generate the project.

Explore the project structure:

The .NET MAUI template creates a basic project structure with the following key files:

`MainPage.xaml`: Contains the XAML code for the main page of your application.

`MainPage.xaml.cs`: Contains the C# code-behind for the main page.

`App.xaml`: Contains application-level resources and settings.

`App.xaml.cs`: Contains the application's entry point and initialization code.

`Platforms`: Contains platform-specific code (if needed) for Android, iOS, macOS, and Windows.

Modify the UI (MainPage.xaml):

Open `MainPage.xaml`. You'll see a basic layout with a `Label` displaying "Welcome to .NET MAUI!"

Replace the content of the `Label` with "Hello, World!"

XML

```
<Label
    Text="Hello, World!"
    VerticalOptions="Center"
    HorizontalOptions="Center" />
```

Run the application:

Select your desired target platform (Android, iOS, macOS, or Windows) from the toolbar.

Click the "Play" button to build and run the application.

You should see a window or simulator displaying "Hello, World!" on your chosen platform.

Congratulations! You've just built your first cross-platform application with .NET MAUI.

Experiment and Explore:

Try changing the `Text` property of the `Label` to display different messages.

Explore the other UI controls available in .NET MAUI (e.g., `Button`, `Entry`, `Image`).

Try running the application on different platforms to see how the UI adapts to each environment.

This simple "Hello, World!" example demonstrates the core principles of .NET MAUI: write your UI code once and deploy it across multiple platforms. As you delve deeper into .NET MAUI, you'll discover its full potential for creating complex and engaging user interfaces.

3.3 Exploring MAUI Essentials: Accessing Device Features Across Platforms

.NET MAUI Essentials is a powerful library that unlocks the potential of your cross-platform applications by providing access to common device features. With MAUI Essentials, you can seamlessly interact with sensors, geolocation, connectivity, and more, all with a unified API that works across Android, iOS, macOS, and Windows.

Why use MAUI Essentials?

Cross-platform Simplicity: Write code once and access device features on any supported platform without worrying about platform-specific APIs.

Increased Functionality: Enhance your applications with features like taking photos, accessing the device's location, using the compass, and more.

Improved User Experience: Create more engaging and interactive applications that respond to the user's environment and provide personalized experiences.

Streamlined Development: MAUI Essentials simplifies common tasks, reducing the amount of code you need to write and making your development process more efficient.

Key features of MAUI Essentials:

Sensors: Access accelerometer, compass, gyroscope, and orientation sensors to detect device movement and orientation.

Geolocation: Get the device's current location, track location changes, and calculate distances.

Connectivity: Check network connectivity, monitor connection changes, and access network information.

Device Information: Retrieve details about the device, such as model, manufacturer, operating system, and screen size.

File System: Read and write files to the device's storage, including application-specific storage and shared storage.

Preferences: Store and retrieve key-value pairs for application settings and user preferences.

Clipboard: Copy and paste text and data to and from the system clipboard.

App Actions: Create shortcuts that allow users to quickly access specific features within your application.

Browser: Open web pages within your application or launch the default web browser.

Phone Dialer: Initiate phone calls from your application.

Email: Compose and send emails.

SMS: Send SMS messages.

Vibration: Trigger device vibrations for notifications or feedback.

Flashlight: Control the device's flashlight (if available).

Share: Share content from your application with other apps.

Text-to-Speech: Convert text to spoken words.

Example: Getting the device's location

Code snippet

```
async void GetLocation()
{
    try
    {
                    var    location    =    await
Geolocation.GetLastKnownLocationAsync();

        if (location != null)
        {
                    Console.WriteLine($"Latitude:
{location.Latitude},                    Longitude:
{location.Longitude},                    Altitude:[22]
{location.Altitude}");
        }
    }
    catch (FeatureNotSupportedException fnsEx)
    {
            // Handle not supported on device
exception
    }
    catch (FeatureNotEnabledException fneEx)
    {
        // Handle not enabled on device exception
    }
    catch (PermissionException pEx)
```

```
    {
        // Handle permission exception
    }
    catch (Exception ex)
    {
        // Unable to get location[23]
    }
}
```

MAUI Essentials empowers you to build feature-rich applications that interact with the user's device in meaningful ways. By leveraging its cross-platform capabilities, you can create engaging and personalized experiences that delight your users.

Chapter 4

Accessing Data and Services

4.1 Working with Databases: Entity Framework Core and Cross-Platform Data Access

Modern applications often rely on databases to store and manage data. Entity Framework Core (EF Core) is a lightweight, cross-platform object-relational mapper (ORM) that simplifies database interactions in .NET applications. It allows you to work with databases using C# objects instead of writing raw SQL queries.

Why use Entity Framework Core?

Increased productivity: EF Core reduces the need to write repetitive SQL code for common data access operations, allowing you to focus on your application's logic.

Code-first approach: Define your database structure using C# classes (entities), and EF Core will generate the database schema for you. This enables a more agile and iterative development workflow.

Cross-platform compatibility: EF Core supports a wide range of databases, including SQL Server, SQLite, MySQL, PostgreSQL, and more, making it suitable for diverse deployment environments.

LINQ support: Use LINQ (Language Integrated Query) to write expressive and type-safe queries against your database.

Change tracking: EF Core automatically tracks changes to your entities, making it easy to persist those changes to the database.

Key concepts in EF Core:

DbContext: Represents a session with the database, providing methods for querying, adding, updating, and deleting data.

Entities: C# classes that map to tables in the database.

Relationships: Define how entities are related to each other (e.g., one-to-many, many-to-many).

Migrations: Enable you to evolve your database schema over time by creating and applying code-based migrations.

Example: Creating a simple data model

Code snippet

```csharp
// Define an entity class
public class Product
{
    public int Id { get; set; }
    public string Name { get; set; }
    public decimal Price { get; set;[1] }
}


// Create a DbContext
public class MyDbContext : DbContext
{
    public DbSet<Product> Products { get; set; }

                protected    override    void
OnConfiguring(DbContextOptionsBuilder[2]
optionsBuilder)
    {
                optionsBuilder.UseSqlite("Data[3]
Source=mydatabase.db");
    }
}
```

Using EF Core for data access:

Code snippet

```csharp
// Create a new instance of the DbContext
using (var db = new MyDbContext())
{
    // Add a new product
    var product = new Product { Name = "Laptop",
Price = 1200 };
    db.Products.Add(product);
    db.SaveChanges();

    // Query for products
    var products = db.Products.Where(p => p.Price
> 1000).ToList();

    // Update a product
    var existingProduct = db.Products.Find(1);
    if (existingProduct != null)
    {
        existingProduct.Price = 1300;
        db.SaveChanges();
    }

    // Delete a product
    db.Products.Remove(product);
    db.SaveChanges();
}
```

EF Core simplifies database interactions, allowing you to focus on your application's logic while providing a robust and efficient way to manage your data.

4.2 Consuming RESTful APIs: Making Web Requests and Handling JSON Data

Modern applications often need to interact with external services and retrieve data from the web. RESTful APIs (Representational State Transfer Application Programming Interfaces) provide a standardized way to access and manipulate data over HTTP. In this section, we'll explore how to consume RESTful APIs in your C# applications, make web requests, and handle JSON data.

What is a RESTful API?

A RESTful API is a web service that adheres to the principles of REST architectural style. It uses standard HTTP methods (GET, POST, PUT, DELETE) to perform operations on resources identified by URLs. Data is typically exchanged in JSON (JavaScript Object Notation) or XML format.

Making web requests with HttpClient

The `HttpClient` class in .NET provides a powerful way to make web requests and interact with RESTful APIs. Here's a basic example of making a GET request:

Code snippet

```
using (var client = new HttpClient())
{
    // Send a GET request to the API endpoint
                var      response      =      await
client.GetAsync("https://api.example.com/data");

    // Check if the request was successful
    if (response.IsSuccessStatusCode)
    {
        // Read the response content as a string
```

```
                             var    content   =    await
response.Content.ReadAsStringAsync();[1]

        // Process the JSON data
        // ...
    }
    else
    {
        // Handle the error
                        Console.WriteLine($"Error:
{response.StatusCode}");
    }
}
```

Handling JSON data with System.Text.Json

The `System.Text.Json` namespace provides classes for
serializing and deserializing JSON data. You can use it to convert
JSON strings to C# objects and vice versa.

Code snippet

```
// Example JSON data
string jsonData = @"
{
  ""name"": ""John Doe"",
  ""age"": 30,
  ""city"": ""New York""
}
";

// Deserialize the JSON data into a C# object
var                    person                    =
JsonSerializer.Deserialize<Person>(jsonData);
```

```
// Access the properties of the object
Console.WriteLine($"Name:   {person.Name},   Age:
{person.Age}, City: {person.City}");

// Serialize a C# object to JSON
string              newJsonData            =
JsonSerializer.Serialize(person);
```

Best practices for consuming RESTful APIs

Use asynchronous methods: Use `async` and `await` keywords for making web requests to avoid blocking the UI thread.

Handle errors: Implement proper error handling to gracefully handle network issues, API errors, and invalid data.

Use appropriate HTTP methods: Choose the correct HTTP method (GET, POST, PUT, DELETE) based on the operation you want to perform.

Secure your API keys: If your API requires authentication, store your API keys securely and avoid hardcoding them in your application.

Follow API documentation: Refer to the API documentation for details on endpoints, request parameters, and response formats.

By mastering these techniques, you can effectively consume RESTful APIs in your C# applications, retrieve data from the web, and integrate with external services.

4.3 Connecting to Cloud Services: Azure Integration and Serverless Functions

Cloud computing has revolutionized how we build and deploy applications.[1] Azure, Microsoft's cloud platform, offers a vast array of services, from virtual machines and databases to serverless functions and AI capabilities. In this section, we'll explore how to integrate your C# applications with Azure and leverage the power of serverless functions.

Why use Azure?

Scalability and Reliability: Azure's infrastructure is designed to handle massive workloads and provide high availability for your applications.

Wide range of services: Azure offers a comprehensive suite of services to meet diverse needs, including compute, storage, networking, databases, AI, and more.

Cost-effectiveness: Pay-as-you-go pricing models allow you to optimize costs and only pay for the resources you consume.[4]

Security and Compliance: Azure adheres to strict security and compliance standards, ensuring the safety and privacy of your data.

Integration with .NET: Azure provides excellent support for .NET applications, with SDKs, tools, and services specifically designed for .NET developers.

Integrating with Azure services

Azure offers SDKs for .NET that provide convenient access to various Azure services. Here are some examples:

Azure Storage: Store and retrieve files, blobs, queues, and tables in Azure Storage.

Azure Cosmos DB: Interact with a globally distributed, multi-model database service.

Azure SQL Database: Connect to a managed SQL Server database in the cloud.

Azure Active Directory: Implement authentication and authorization for your applications.

Example: Uploading a file to Azure Blob Storage

Code snippet

```
// Install the Azure.Storage.Blobs NuGet package

// Connection string to your Azure Storage
account
string               connectionString          =
"YOUR_CONNECTION_STRING";

// Create a BlobServiceClient
BlobServiceClient    blobServiceClient    =    new
BlobServiceClient(connectionString);

// Get a reference to the container
BlobContainerClient      containerClient         =
blobServiceClient.GetBlobContainerClient("myconta
iner");[12]

// Upload a file to the container
using          (var          fileStream          =
File.OpenRead("myfile.txt"))
{
                                              await
containerClient.UploadBlobAsync("myfile.txt",
fileStream);
}
```

Serverless functions with Azure Functions

Azure Functions allow you to run event-driven code without managing infrastructure.[13] You can write functions in C# and deploy them to Azure, where they will be executed in response to triggers like HTTP requests, timer events, or messages from queues.[14]

Example: Creating an HTTP-triggered function

Code snippet

```
//                      Install                  the
Microsoft.Azure.Functions.Worker.Http        NuGet
package

// Define an HTTP-triggered function
[Function("MyHttpTrigger")]
public          static              HttpResponseData
Run([HttpTrigger(AuthorizationLevel.Anonymous,
"get", "post")] HttpRequestData req)
{
    // Get the request body
          string    requestBody    =   await    new
StreamReader(req.Body).ReadToEndAsync();

    // Process the request
          string    responseBody    =    $"Hello,
{requestBody}!";

    // Create a response
                    var        response        =
req.CreateResponse(HttpStatusCode.OK);
          response.Headers.Add("Content-Type",
"text/plain; charset=utf-8");
    response.WriteString(responseBody);[15]

    return response;
}
```

By integrating with Azure and leveraging serverless functions, you can build scalable, resilient, and cost-effective cloud applications.

Chapter 5

Developing Cross-Platform Mobile Applications

5.1 Building Mobile Apps with .NET MAUI: iOS, Android, and Beyond

.NET MAUI empowers you to create stunning native mobile apps that run seamlessly on iOS and Android devices, and even extend to other platforms like Tizen. With a single codebase, you can build user interfaces with native performance, leverage platform-specific features, and reach a broad audience with your mobile applications.

Why choose .NET MAUI for mobile development?

Single codebase, multiple platforms: Write your UI and logic once in C# and XAML, and deploy it to both iOS and Android without maintaining separate codebases. This significantly reduces development time and effort.

Native performance: .NET MAUI utilizes native UI controls, ensuring that your apps look, feel, and perform like native apps on each platform. This provides a superior user experience compared to hybrid or web-based approaches.

Access to platform-specific features: Leverage .NET MAUI's platform-specific APIs to access device features like cameras, sensors, and geolocation. This allows you to create apps that deeply integrate with the mobile device's capabilities.

Modern architecture: .NET MAUI is built on the modern .NET 6 framework, providing access to performance improvements, new features, and a robust ecosystem of libraries and tools.

Simplified development: .NET MAUI streamlines the development process with features like hot reload, live visual tree, and XAML IntelliSense, making it easier to build and debug your mobile apps.

Key considerations for mobile development with .NET MAUI:

UI design: Design your UI with a mobile-first approach, considering the smaller screen sizes and touch interactions of mobile devices.

Navigation: Implement intuitive navigation patterns that allow users to easily move between different screens and sections of your app.

Performance optimization: Optimize your app's performance by minimizing resource usage, reducing UI complexity, and utilizing asynchronous operations.

Platform-specific adaptations: While .NET MAUI promotes code sharing, be prepared to make platform-specific adaptations for UI elements, device features, or platform-specific guidelines.

Testing and debugging: Thoroughly test your app on both iOS and Android devices and emulators to ensure compatibility and identify potential issues.

Extending to other platforms

.NET MAUI's flexibility allows you to extend your mobile apps to other platforms like Tizen, a versatile operating system used in various devices, including TVs, wearables, and appliances. This opens up new possibilities for reaching a wider audience with your .NET MAUI applications.

By combining .NET MAUI's cross-platform capabilities with platform-specific optimizations, you can create high-quality mobile apps that delight users on iOS, Android, and beyond.

5.2 Mobile-Specific UI Design: Adapting to Different Screen Sizes and Orientations

Mobile devices come in a wide array of screen sizes and aspect ratios. Users also frequently rotate their devices between portrait and landscape orientations. Designing user interfaces that adapt seamlessly to these variations is crucial for creating a positive user experience.

Challenges of mobile UI design

Diverse screen sizes: From small smartphones to large tablets, your app needs to look and function correctly on a variety of screen dimensions.

Varying aspect ratios: Different devices have different screen proportions (e.g., 16:9, 4:3), which can affect the layout and presentation of your UI elements.

Orientation changes: Users can rotate their devices between portrait and landscape modes. Your UI should adjust gracefully to these changes, ensuring that content remains accessible and readable.

Touch input: Mobile UIs are primarily interacted with through touch. Design elements should be appropriately sized and spaced for easy touch targeting.

Strategies for adaptive UI design

Responsive layouts: Use layout mechanisms that dynamically adjust to different screen sizes and orientations. .NET MAUI provides flexible layout controls like `Grid`, `StackLayout`, and `FlexLayout` to help you create responsive UIs.

Adaptive scaling: Scale images and other visual elements appropriately to maintain their proportions and clarity on different screen sizes.

Orientation-aware design: Consider both portrait and landscape orientations when designing your UI. Reposition or resize elements as needed to ensure optimal usability in both modes.

Fluid grids and flexible images: Use CSS media queries and flexible image techniques to adapt the layout and size of elements based on screen dimensions.

Touch-friendly elements: Ensure that buttons, icons, and other interactive elements are large enough and have sufficient spacing for easy touch targeting.

.NET MAUI features for adaptive UI

Layout options: .NET MAUI offers a variety of layout controls (`Grid`, `StackLayout`, `FlexLayout`, `AbsoluteLayout`, `RelativeLayout`) that provide flexibility in arranging UI elements.

Platform-specific adjustments: You can use platform-specific code or conditional XAML to make adjustments to the UI based on the platform or device characteristics.

VisualStateManager: Define different visual states for your UI elements and trigger them based on screen size, orientation, or other factors.

OnIdiom and OnPlatform: These XAML markup extensions allow you to specify different properties or resources based on the device's idiom (phone, tablet, desktop) or platform (iOS, Android, Windows).

Example: Using Grid for responsive layout

XML

```xml
<Grid>
    <Grid.RowDefinitions>
        <RowDefinition Height="Auto" />
        <RowDefinition Height="*" />
```

```
    </Grid.RowDefinitions>

    <Label Text="Header" Grid.Row="0" />
    <ListView Grid.Row="1">
        </ListView>
</Grid>
```

In this example, the `Grid` layout divides the screen into two rows. The first row contains a header with `Height="Auto"`, ensuring it takes up only the necessary space. The second row contains a `ListView` with `Height="*"`, allowing it to fill the remaining space. This layout will adapt to different screen sizes and orientations, ensuring that the header remains visible and the list fills the available area.

By implementing these techniques and leveraging .NET MAUI's features, you can create mobile apps that adapt seamlessly to different screen sizes and orientations, providing a consistent and enjoyable user experience across a wide range of devices.

5.3 Publishing Your Mobile Apps: App Store and Google Play Deployment

You've built your amazing mobile app with .NET MAUI, and now it's time to share it with the world! Publishing your app on the App Store (for iOS) and Google Play (for Android) involves several steps to ensure your app meets quality standards and reaches your target audience.

App Store Deployment (iOS)

Enroll in the Apple Developer Program: You'll need an Apple Developer account to publish apps on the App Store. This requires an annual fee and provides access to development tools, resources, and distribution channels.

Prepare your app for submission:

App metadata: Gather information like your app's name, description, keywords, screenshots, and promotional materials.

Code signing: Obtain the necessary certificates and provisioning profiles to digitally sign your app, ensuring its authenticity and integrity.

App Store Connect: Create an app record in App Store Connect, providing details about your app and configuring its settings.

Build and archive your app: Use Xcode to build an archive of your app, which is a package containing all the necessary files for distribution.

Upload your app to App Store Connect: Submit your app archive through Xcode or Transporter, a tool for uploading app packages to App Store Connect.

Complete the app submission process: Fill in the remaining information in App Store Connect, including pricing, age rating, and export compliance.

Submit for review: Once you've completed all the necessary steps, submit your app for review by Apple. The review process may take a few days, and Apple will notify you of the outcome.

Release your app: If your app is approved, you can release it on the App Store, making it available to users worldwide.

Google Play Deployment (Android)

Create a Google Play Developer account: You'll need a Google Play Developer account to publish apps on Google Play. This requires a one-time registration fee.

Prepare your app for submission:

App metadata: Gather information like your app's title, description, screenshots, and promotional graphics.

Signing your app: Generate a signing key to digitally sign your app, ensuring its authenticity and preventing tampering.

Google Play Console: Create an app listing in the Google Play Console, providing details about your app and configuring its settings.

Build and sign your app: Use Visual Studio or the .NET CLI to build a release version of your app and sign it with your signing key.

Upload your app bundle to Google Play Console: Upload your app bundle (`.aab` file) to the Google Play Console. App bundles are optimized for different device configurations, reducing the download size for users.

Complete the app submission process: Fill in the remaining information in the Google Play Console, including content rating, pricing, and distribution settings.

Rollout your release: Choose a release type (internal testing, closed testing, open testing, production) and gradually roll out your app to users.

Monitor your app's performance: Track your app's downloads, ratings, reviews, and crashes in the Google Play Console to identify areas for improvement.

Tips for successful app publishing

Follow platform guidelines: Adhere to the App Store Review Guidelines and Google Play Developer Policy Center to ensure your app meets quality standards and avoids rejection.

Test thoroughly: Test your app on various devices and emulators to identify and fix any bugs or compatibility issues.

Optimize for discoverability: Use relevant keywords, compelling descriptions, and high-quality screenshots to improve your app's visibility in app stores.

Engage with users: Respond to user reviews, address issues promptly, and continuously update your app to provide a positive user experience.

By following these steps and best practices, you can successfully publish your .NET MAUI mobile apps on the App Store and Google Play, making them available to millions of users worldwide.

Chapter 6

Creating Cross-Platform Desktop Applications

6.1 Desktop Development with .NET MAUI: Windows, macOS, and Linux

.NET MAUI isn't just for mobile! It extends its cross-platform prowess to the desktop, enabling you to build native applications for Windows, macOS, and even Linux. This means you can leverage your C# and .NET skills to create desktop experiences that are performant, visually appealing, and consistent across different operating systems.

Why choose .NET MAUI for desktop development?

Single codebase, multiple platforms: Write your UI and application logic once, and deploy it to Windows, macOS, and Linux with minimal platform-specific adjustments. This significantly reduces development time and effort compared to maintaining separate codebases for each platform.

Native performance and look and feel: .NET MAUI utilizes the native UI frameworks of each operating system, ensuring that your desktop applications look and feel like they belong on the target platform. This provides a superior user experience compared to web-based or cross-platform solutions that rely on generic UI rendering.

Access to platform-specific APIs: .NET MAUI allows you to access platform-specific APIs and features, enabling you to integrate deeply with the operating system and provide a richer user experience.

Modern architecture: Built on .NET 6, .NET MAUI benefits from the latest performance improvements, language features, and a vast ecosystem of libraries and tools.

Integration with existing .NET libraries: Leverage your existing .NET libraries and code in your .NET MAUI desktop applications, maximizing code reuse and reducing development time.

Key considerations for desktop development with .NET MAUI:

Windowing and menus: .NET MAUI provides APIs for managing windows, menus, and dialogs, allowing you to create desktop applications with standard windowing behavior.

Desktop-specific UI controls: Utilize .NET MAUI's controls that are specifically designed for desktop environments, such as `MenuBar`, `TrayIcon`, and `ContextMenu`.

File system access: Access the file system to read and write files, interact with directories, and manage application data.

Interoperability with native libraries: If needed, you can interop with native libraries on each platform to access specialized functionalities.

Deployment and packaging: .NET MAUI provides tools and options for packaging and deploying your desktop applications to different operating systems.

Example: Creating a simple window with a menu

Code snippet

```
// Create a new window
var window = new Window()
{
    Title = "My Desktop App",
    Page = new ContentPage
    {
```

```csharp
        Content = new Label { Text = "Hello from
.NET MAUI!" }
    }
};

// Create a menu bar
var menuBar = new MenuBar();
var fileMenu = new Menu("File");
fileMenu.Add(new MenuItem { Text = "Exit",
Command = new Command(() => {
Application.Current.Quit(); }) });
menuBar.Add(fileMenu);

// Set the menu bar for the window
window.MenuBar = menuBar;

// Show the window
Application.Current.OpenWindow(window);
```

.NET MAUI expands the horizons of cross-platform development, allowing you to create not only mobile apps but also native desktop experiences for Windows, macOS, and Linux with a single, unified codebase.

6.2 Using Native APIs and Platform-Specific Features

While .NET MAUI excels at providing a unified cross-platform development experience, there are times when you need to tap into the unique capabilities of each platform. This is where accessing native APIs and platform-specific features becomes essential.

Why use native APIs?

Access specialized functionalities: Native APIs provide access to features that might not be available in the cross-platform .NET MAUI framework. This could include functionalities like accessing specific hardware sensors, interacting with platform-specific UI elements, or utilizing operating system services.

Enhance performance: In some cases, using native APIs can offer performance advantages compared to cross-platform abstractions. This is particularly relevant for computationally intensive tasks or when interacting with low-level system components.

Integrate with existing native libraries: If you have existing native libraries or code, you can integrate them into your .NET MAUI application using platform channels or other interoperability mechanisms.

Approaches to accessing native APIs

Platform channels: .NET MAUI provides a mechanism called platform channels that allows you to invoke native code from your shared C# code. You define an interface in your shared code and implement it separately for each platform using the native language (e.g., Swift or Objective-C for iOS, Java or Kotlin for Android).

.NET MAUI Essentials: While .NET MAUI Essentials provides cross-platform abstractions for many common features, it also offers platform-specific APIs for accessing more specialized functionalities.

Third-party libraries: Numerous third-party libraries provide .NET bindings for native APIs, making it easier to integrate with platform-specific features.

Conditional compilation: Use conditional compilation directives (#if __IOS__, #if __ANDROID__, etc.) to include platform-specific code blocks in your shared code.

Example: Accessing the device's battery level (platform channels)

Define an interface in shared code:

Code snippet

```
public interface IBattery
{
    int GetBatteryLevel();
}
```

Implement the interface on each platform:

iOS (Swift):

Swift

```
public class BatteryImplementation : NSObject,
IBattery {
    public func getBatteryLevel() -> Int {

UIDevice.current.isBatteryMonitoringEnabled    =
true
        return Int(UIDevice.current.batteryLevel
* 100)
    }
}
```

Android (Java):

Java

```java
public class BatteryImplementation implements IBattery {
    @Override
    public int getBatteryLevel() {
        Intent batteryIntent = MainActivity.this.registerReceiver(null, new IntentFilter(Intent.ACTION_BATTERY_CHANGED));
        int level = batteryIntent.getIntExtra(BatteryManager.EXTRA_LEVEL,[1] -1);
        int scale = batteryIntent.getIntExtra(BatteryManager.EXTRA_SCALE, -1);[2]
        return (int) ((level / (float) scale) * 100);
    }
}
```

Register the platform-specific implementations:

Code snippet

```
// In your MauiProgram.cs
builder.Services.AddSingleton<IBattery>(Battery.D
efault);
```

Use the interface in your shared code:

Code snippet

```
// In your ViewModel or Code-behind
var battery = DependencyService.Get<IBattery>();
int batteryLevel = battery.GetBatteryLevel();
```

By combining the power of .NET MAUI's cross-platform framework with the flexibility of accessing native APIs, you can create applications that are truly tailored to each platform, providing a richer and more engaging user experience.

6.3 Packaging and Distributing Desktop Applications

Once you've built your impressive desktop application with .NET MAUI, it's time to package it up and distribute it to your users. This involves bundling your application and its dependencies into an installer or executable that can be easily installed and run on different operating systems.

Why is proper packaging important?

Ease of installation: A well-packaged application provides a smooth and user-friendly installation experience, minimizing confusion and frustration for your users.

Dependency management: The package includes all the necessary dependencies and runtime components, ensuring that your application runs correctly on target machines without requiring users to install anything extra.

Professional presentation: A polished installer or executable enhances the perceived quality of your application and gives it a more professional look.

Security: Packaging can include digital signatures to verify the authenticity of your application and protect it from tampering.

Updates: Packaging can facilitate updates, allowing you to deliver new features and bug fixes to your users seamlessly.

Packaging options for .NET MAUI desktop applications

MSIX (Windows): The modern packaging format for Windows applications. MSIX provides a reliable installation experience, clean uninstallation, and automatic updates. .NET MAUI integrates well with MSIX, allowing you to create MSIX packages for your Windows applications.

macOS app bundles: The standard format for distributing applications on macOS. .NET MAUI can generate app bundles that can be distributed through the Mac App Store or directly to users.

Linux packages (DEB, RPM): For Linux, you can create distribution-specific packages like DEB (Debian) or RPM (Red Hat) to facilitate installation on different Linux distributions.

Distribution channels

Direct download: Make your application available for download from your website or other online platforms.

App stores: Publish your application on platform-specific app stores like the Microsoft Store (Windows) or Mac App Store (macOS).

Package managers: On Linux, you can distribute your application through package managers like APT (Debian) or YUM (Red Hat).

Steps for packaging and distributing your .NET MAUI desktop application

Choose the appropriate packaging format: Select the packaging format that best suits your target operating system(s) and distribution strategy.

Configure your project: Set up your .NET MAUI project to generate the desired package format. This may involve configuring project properties, adding platform-specific settings, or using command-line tools.

Build your application: Build a release version of your application, ensuring that all dependencies are included and optimizations are enabled.

Create the package: Use the appropriate tools to create the package (e.g., Visual Studio for MSIX, `dotnet publish` for macOS app bundles).

Test the installation: Thoroughly test the installation process on different machines to ensure it works smoothly and all dependencies are correctly installed.

Distribute your application: Choose your preferred distribution channel and make your application available to your users.

By carefully packaging and distributing your .NET MAUI desktop applications, you can ensure a positive user

experience, reach a wider audience, and present your software in a professional manner.

Chapter 7

Testing and Debugging Cross-Platform Applications

7.1 Unit Testing and Test-Driven Development in C#

Testing is a critical aspect of software development, ensuring that your code behaves as expected and remains reliable as your application evolves. Unit testing, in particular, focuses on testing individual units of code (like methods or classes) in isolation. Test-Driven Development (TDD) takes this a step further by writing tests *before* writing the code, using the tests to guide the development process.

Why Unit Test?

Find bugs early: Unit tests help you identify and fix bugs early in the development cycle, when they are easier and cheaper to address.

Improve code quality: Writing testable code often leads to better design, with more modular and loosely coupled components.

Facilitate refactoring: Unit tests provide a safety net when refactoring code, giving you confidence that your changes haven't broken existing functionality.

Document code behavior: Unit tests serve as living documentation, demonstrating how your code is intended to be used.

Test-Driven Development (TDD)

TDD follows a simple cycle:

Red: Write a failing unit test for the functionality you want to add.

Green: Write the minimum amount of code to make the test pass.

Refactor: Improve the code while ensuring the tests still pass.

This iterative approach ensures that your code is thoroughly tested and that you only write code that is necessary to meet the requirements.

Unit Testing Frameworks in C#

xUnit: A popular, extensible testing framework.

NUnit: Another widely used framework with a rich feature set.

MSTest: Microsoft's testing framework, often integrated with Visual Studio.

Example using xUnit:

Code snippet

```csharp
// Code to be tested
public class Calculator
{
    public int Add(int a, int b)
    {
        return a + b;
    }
}

// Unit test
public class CalculatorTests
{
    [Fact]
    public void Add_ShouldReturnCorrectSum()
```

```
    {
        // Arrange
        var calculator = new Calculator();

        // Act
        var result = calculator.Add(2, 3);

        // Assert
        Assert.Equal(5, result);
    }
}
```

Key Concepts in Unit Testing

Arrange: Set up the necessary objects and data for the test.

Act: Execute the code being tested.

Assert: Verify that the result meets the expected outcome.

Test naming: Use descriptive names for your test methods that clearly indicate what is being tested.

Code coverage: Aim for high code coverage, meaning that a large portion of your code is executed by your tests.

Benefits of TDD

Higher code quality: TDD leads to more modular, testable, and maintainable code.

Reduced bug count: By writing tests first, you are more likely to catch bugs early.

Increased confidence: Having a comprehensive suite of unit tests gives you confidence to make changes to your code.

Improved design: TDD encourages you to think about the design of your code before you start writing it.

By incorporating unit testing and TDD into your C# development workflow, you can significantly improve the quality, reliability, and maintainability of your applications.

7.2 Debugging Techniques for Cross-Platform Code

Debugging is an essential skill for any developer, and it becomes even more crucial when working with cross-platform code. Since your application runs on different operating systems and environments, you need to be equipped with techniques that help you identify and resolve issues across these diverse platforms.

Challenges of debugging cross-platform code

Different environments: Your code might behave differently on different operating systems, making it challenging to pinpoint the source of a bug.

Platform-specific issues: Some bugs might be specific to a particular platform due to differences in operating system versions, hardware, or native libraries.

Debugging tools: While some debugging tools are cross-platform, others might be specific to a particular operating system or IDE.

Debugging techniques for cross-platform code

Logging:

Use a logging framework (like NLog or Serilog) to record information about your application's execution.

Include platform-specific information in your logs, such as operating system version, device model, etc.

Use different log levels (debug, info, warning, error) to filter and prioritize log messages.

Debugging tools:

Visual Studio: A powerful IDE with excellent debugging capabilities for .NET applications on Windows and macOS. It supports remote debugging for other platforms.

Visual Studio Code: A lightweight and versatile code editor with debugging support for various languages and platforms.

Platform-specific debuggers: Use debuggers like Xcode (iOS) or Android Studio (Android) for platform-specific debugging.

Browser developer tools: For web-based applications, use browser developer tools to debug JavaScript code and inspect network requests.

Testing on multiple platforms:

Regularly test your application on different operating systems, devices, and emulators to identify platform-specific issues early on.

Use automated testing frameworks to run tests across multiple platforms.

Conditional breakpoints:

Set breakpoints in your code that are triggered only under specific conditions, such as a particular operating system or device.

Remote debugging:

Use remote debugging tools to connect to your application running on a different machine or device. This allows you to debug code running in a different environment.

Platform-specific code inspection:

When facing a platform-specific issue, carefully inspect the code that interacts with native APIs or platform-specific features.

Use platform-specific debugging tools to step through the native code if necessary.

Isolate the issue:

Try to reproduce the bug in a minimal example to isolate the problematic code and eliminate external factors.

Consult documentation and communities:

Refer to platform-specific documentation and online communities for solutions to common problems or known issues.

Example: Using conditional breakpoints in Visual Studio

Set a breakpoint in your code.

Right-click on the breakpoint and select "Conditions...".

Enter a condition that evaluates to true when you want the breakpoint to be hit (e.g., `Environment.OSVersion.Platform == PlatformID.Win32NT`).

By mastering these debugging techniques and utilizing the right tools, you can effectively troubleshoot issues in your cross-platform code and ensure that your application runs smoothly across different environments.

7.3 Performance Optimization and Profiling

Performance is paramount in software development. Users expect applications to be responsive, efficient, and consume minimal resources. Performance optimization involves identifying bottlenecks in your code and applying techniques to improve its speed and efficiency. Profiling tools help you analyze your application's performance and pinpoint areas that need optimization.

Why optimize performance?

Enhanced user experience: Fast and responsive applications provide a better user experience, leading to increased satisfaction and engagement.

Reduced resource consumption: Optimized applications consume less memory, CPU, and battery power, which is crucial for mobile devices and resource-constrained environments.

Improved scalability: Performance optimization allows your application to handle larger workloads and more users without sacrificing responsiveness.

Cost savings: Efficient applications can reduce infrastructure costs by requiring fewer servers or resources.

Performance optimization techniques

Identify bottlenecks: Use profiling tools to pinpoint the parts of your code that consume the most time or resources.

Optimize algorithms and data structures: Choose efficient algorithms and data structures that are well-suited to the task at hand.

Reduce memory allocations: Minimize the creation of new objects and utilize object pooling to reuse existing objects.

Asynchronous programming: Use asynchronous operations (`async` and `await`) to avoid blocking the main thread and improve responsiveness.

Caching: Store frequently accessed data in a cache to reduce redundant computations or data retrieval.

Lazy loading: Load data or resources only when they are needed, rather than upfront.

Optimize database queries: Use efficient database queries and indexing to minimize data access time.

Minimize network requests: Reduce the number of network requests and optimize data transfer size.

Profiling: Regularly profile your application to identify new performance bottlenecks as your code evolves.

Profiling tools

Visual Studio Profiler: Built into Visual Studio, it provides detailed performance analysis, including CPU usage, memory allocation, and call stacks.

.NET CLI tools: The `dotnet trace` command-line tool allows you to collect performance traces and analyze them with tools like PerfView.

Performance Counters: Monitor system-level performance metrics like CPU usage, memory usage, and disk I/O.

Third-party profiling tools: Explore specialized profiling tools like dotTrace and ANTS Performance Profiler for advanced analysis and optimization.

Example: Analyzing CPU usage with Visual Studio Profiler

In Visual Studio, go to "Debug" -> "Performance Profiler...".

Select "CPU Usage" and click "Start."

Run your application and perform the actions you want to analyze.

Stop the profiler and examine the results. The profiler will show you which functions consume the most CPU time, allowing you to focus your optimization efforts.

By combining performance optimization techniques with profiling tools, you can identify and address performance bottlenecks in your C# code, resulting in faster, more efficient, and more scalable applications.

Chapter 8

Advanced Topics in Cross-Platform Development

8.1 Working with Asynchronous Programming and Multithreading

Modern applications often need to handle tasks that take a significant amount of time, such as network requests, file I/O, or complex calculations. Asynchronous programming and multithreading provide powerful ways to manage these long-running operations without blocking the main thread and keeping your application responsive.

Asynchronous Programming

Asynchronous programming allows you to execute code without waiting for it to complete, freeing up the current thread to perform other tasks. In C#, you can use the `async` and `await` keywords to write asynchronous methods.

`async` **keyword:** Marks a method as asynchronous, enabling the use of `await` within it.

`await` **keyword:** Asynchronously waits for a task to complete without blocking the current thread.

Example:

Code snippet

```
public                async                Task<string>
DownloadWebsiteContent(string url)
{
```

```
    using (var client = new HttpClient())
    {
        // Await the asynchronous operation
                        var    content    =    await
client.GetStringAsync(url);
        return content;
    }
}
```

Benefits of asynchronous programming:

Improved responsiveness: Avoids blocking the main thread, keeping the UI responsive.

Enhanced performance: Allows for concurrent execution of tasks, potentially improving overall performance.

Simplified code: Makes asynchronous code easier to read and write compared to traditional callback-based approaches.

Multithreading

Multithreading allows you to execute multiple threads of execution concurrently within a single application. Each thread can perform a different task, enabling parallel processing and potentially improving performance.

`Thread` **class:** Represents a thread of execution.

`Task` **class:** Represents an asynchronous operation that can be run on a separate thread.

Example:

Code snippet

```
// Create a new thread
Thread thread = new Thread(() =>
```

```
{
    // Perform a long-running task
        Console.WriteLine("Hello  from  a  separate
thread!");
});

// Start the thread
thread.Start();
```

Benefits of multithreading:

Parallel processing: Enables execution of multiple tasks simultaneously, potentially improving performance for CPU-bound operations.

Improved responsiveness: Can be used to offload long-running tasks to background threads, keeping the UI responsive.

Choosing between asynchronous programming and multithreading

Asynchronous programming: Preferable for I/O-bound operations (e.g., network requests, file I/O) where the thread spends most of its time waiting for external resources.

Multithreading: More suitable for CPU-bound operations (e.g., complex calculations, image processing) where the thread is actively performing computations.

Important considerations

Thread safety: When using multithreading, be mindful of thread safety issues, such as race conditions and deadlocks. Use synchronization mechanisms (e.g., locks, mutexes) to protect shared resources.

Context switching: Excessive thread creation and context switching can introduce overhead and negatively impact performance.

Debugging: Debugging multithreaded applications can be more challenging due to the concurrent execution of multiple threads.

By understanding and utilizing asynchronous programming and multithreading effectively, you can create responsive, efficient, and high-performance C# applications that handle complex tasks with ease.

8.2 Implementing Security Best Practices in Your Applications

Security should be a top priority in every stage of software development. Building secure applications protects user data, maintains your reputation, and prevents costly breaches. Here's a breakdown of essential security practices to implement in your C# and .NET applications:

1. Authentication and Authorization

Strong passwords: Enforce strong password policies, requiring complexity, length, and regular updates.

Multi-factor authentication (MFA): Add an extra layer of security by requiring users to provide multiple forms of authentication[1] (e.g., password and one-time code).

Role-based access control (RBAC): Limit user access to specific resources and functionalities based on their roles and permissions.

OAuth 2.0 and OpenID Connect: Use industry-standard protocols for secure authentication and authorization.

Azure Active Directory: Leverage Azure AD for identity management and authentication services.

2. Data Protection

Encryption: Encrypt sensitive data both in transit (using HTTPS) and at rest (using encryption algorithms).

Data validation: Validate all user input to prevent injection attacks (e.g., SQL injection, cross-site scripting).

Secure storage: Store sensitive data securely, such as API keys, passwords, and connection strings. Use secure storage mechanisms like Azure Key Vault.

Data masking: Mask or redact sensitive data when displaying it to users.

Regular backups: Implement regular backups of your data to prevent data loss in case of a security incident.

3. Secure Coding Practices

Input validation: Validate all user input to prevent injection attacks and ensure data integrity.

Output encoding: Encode output to prevent cross-site scripting (XSS) vulnerabilities.

Parameterization: Use parameterized queries to prevent SQL injection attacks.

Least privilege principle: Grant only the necessary permissions to users and applications.

Secure coding guidelines: Follow secure coding guidelines and best practices to prevent common vulnerabilities.

4. Security Auditing and Monitoring

Regular security audits: Conduct regular security audits to identify vulnerabilities and assess your security posture.

Penetration testing: Simulate attacks to identify weaknesses in your application's security.

Logging and monitoring: Log security-related events and monitor your application for suspicious activity.

Vulnerability scanning: Use automated tools to scan your code for known vulnerabilities.

Incident response plan: Develop an incident response plan to handle security breaches effectively.

5. Third-Party Libraries and Dependencies

Secure libraries: Use well-maintained and secure third-party libraries.

Dependency management: Keep your dependencies up-to-date to patch known vulnerabilities.

Vulnerability scanning: Scan your dependencies for vulnerabilities using tools like OWASP Dependency-Check.

6. Deployment and Infrastructure Security

Secure deployment: Use secure deployment practices, such as automated deployments and secure pipelines.

Firewall and network security: Implement firewalls and network security measures to protect your infrastructure.

Secure configurations: Configure your servers and applications securely to minimize vulnerabilities.

Regular updates and patches: Keep your operating systems, software, and libraries up-to-date with the latest security patches.

By implementing these security best practices throughout the development lifecycle, you can create C# and .NET applications that are resilient to attacks, protect user data, and maintain a strong security posture.

8.3 Internationalization and Localization for Global Audiences

Creating applications that cater to a global audience involves more than just translating text.Internationalization and localization are essential processes for ensuring your software is accessible, usable, and culturally relevant to users around the world.

Internationalization (i18n)

Internationalization is the process of designing and developing your application in a way that makes it easy to adapt to different languages, regions, and cultures *without requiring code changes*.It's about building a foundation that supports localization efforts.

Key aspects of internationalization:

Unicode support: Use Unicode encoding to represent text in various languages.

Culture-neutral code: Avoid hardcoding culture-specific assumptions (e.g., date and time formats, currency symbols) in your code.

Externalize resources: Store text, images, and other resources separately from your code, allowing them to be easily translated and localized.

Flexible layouts: Design layouts that can accommodate text expansion and different reading directions.

Locale awareness: Make your application aware of the user's locale (language and region) to provide appropriate formatting and content.

Localization (l10n)

Localization is the process of adapting your application to a specific target market. This involves translating text, adjusting date and time formats, using appropriate currency symbols, and incorporating cultural nuances.

Key aspects of localization:

Translation: Translate all user-facing text, including menus, labels, error messages, and documentation.

Date and time formats: Use culturally appropriate date and time formats.

Number formats: Use correct decimal separators, grouping separators, and currency symbols.

Cultural considerations: Adapt images, colors, and other visual elements to align with cultural preferences.

Legal and regulatory compliance: Ensure your application complies with local laws and regulations.

.NET MAUI features for internationalization and localization

Resource files: .NET MAUI supports resource files (.resx) for storing localized strings and other resources.

Culture settings: You can set the culture of your application to use appropriate locale-specific formatting.

XAML localization extensions: Use XAML markup extensions like `x:Uid` to mark elements for localization.

Third-party libraries: Leverage libraries like `I18NPortable` for advanced localization features.

Best practices

Plan for localization early: Consider internationalization and localization from the beginning of the development process.

Use a consistent terminology: Maintain a glossary of terms to ensure consistency across translations.

Test with real users: Conduct testing with native speakers to identify potential issues and ensure cultural appropriateness.

Use professional translation services: For high-quality translations, consider using professional translation services.

By implementing internationalization and localization effectively, you can create applications that cater to a global audience, providing a positive user experience and increasing your reach in international markets.

Chapter 9

Building Cross-Platform Games with C# and .NET

9.1 Introduction to Game Development with .NET and Game Engines

Game development is a fascinating and rewarding field that combines creativity, technology, and storytelling. While C# and .NET might not be the first things that come to mind when you think of game development, they offer a powerful and versatile platform for building a wide range of games, from simple 2D games to complex 3D simulations.

Why use .NET for game development?

C# language: C# is a modern, object-oriented language with a clear syntax and powerful features. It's easy to learn and use, making it a great choice for both beginner and experienced game developers.

Performance: .NET 6 and later versions offer excellent performance, thanks to optimizations in the runtime and garbage collection. This allows you to create games that run smoothly and efficiently.

Cross-platform capabilities: .NET supports multiple platforms, including Windows, macOS, Linux, iOS, and Android. This allows you to reach a wider audience with your games.

Rich ecosystem: .NET has a vast ecosystem of libraries and tools that can be leveraged for game development, including libraries for graphics, audio, physics, and networking.

Strong community: The .NET community is large and active, providing support, resources, and a wealth of knowledge for game developers.

Game engines for .NET

While you can build a game from scratch using .NET libraries, game engines provide a framework and tools that simplify many aspects of game development. Here are some popular game engines that work well with .NET:

Unity: A widely used game engine that supports C# as its scripting language. Unity offers a visual editor, a large asset store, and a strong community. It's a great choice for both 2D and 3D games.

MonoGame: An open-source framework that implements the XNA framework API. MonoGame allows you to create 2D games that can be deployed to various platforms, including Windows, macOS, Linux, iOS, Android, and more.

Stride (formerly Xenko): A powerful open-source game engine with a focus on 3D graphics and visual scripting. It supports C# as its primary scripting language and offers a wide range of features for creating high-fidelity games.

Wave Engine: A .NET-based game engine with a focus on 2D and 3D game development. It offers a visual editor, a component-based architecture, and support for various platforms.

CRYENGINE: A high-fidelity game engine used for creating AAA games. It offers a C# framework that allows you to develop gameplay logic using C#.

Choosing a game engine

The choice of game engine depends on your specific needs and preferences. Consider factors like:

2D vs. 3D: Do you want to create 2D or 3D games?

Ease of use: How easy is the engine to learn and use?

Features: Does the engine offer the features you need for your game (e.g., physics, networking, animation)?

Platform support: Which platforms does the engine support?

Community and support: Is there a strong community and good documentation available?

Licensing: Is the engine open-source, commercially licensed, or has a royalty-based model?

By combining the power of .NET with a suitable game engine, you can unlock your creativity and build engaging and immersive game experiences.

9.2 Building a Simple 2D Game with C# and a Cross-Platform Library

Let's get our hands dirty and build a simple 2D game using C# and a cross-platform library! We'll create a classic "Pong" game where two paddles bounce a ball back and forth. This example will demonstrate the basic concepts of game development, including game loop, input handling, collision detection, and rendering.

Choosing a library

For this example, we'll use **MonoGame**, an open-source, cross-platform framework that implements the XNA framework API. MonoGame allows us to create 2D games that can be deployed to various platforms.

Setting up MonoGame

Install the MonoGame SDK: Download and install the MonoGame SDK from the official website (monogame.net).

Create a new MonoGame project: In Visual Studio, create a new "MonoGame Windows Project" (or a project for your desired platform).

Game structure

Our Pong game will have the following components:

Game loop: A loop that continuously updates the game state and renders the game scene.

Paddles: Two paddles controlled by the players.

Ball: A ball that bounces between the paddles and the walls.

Collision detection: Logic to detect collisions between the ball and the paddles/walls.

Scoring: Keeping track of the score for each player.

Rendering: Drawing the game elements on the screen.

Code example (simplified)

Code snippet

```
// Game1.cs
using Microsoft.Xna.Framework;
using Microsoft.Xna.Framework.Graphics;
using Microsoft.Xna.Framework.Input;

public class Game1 : Game[1]
{
    private GraphicsDeviceManager _graphics;
    private SpriteBatch _spriteBatch;
    private Texture2D _paddleTexture;
    private Texture2D _ballTexture;[2]
    private Vector2 _leftPaddlePosition;
    private Vector2 _rightPaddlePosition;
    private Vector2 _ballPosition;
    private Vector2 _ballVelocity;

    public Game1()
    {
```

```csharp
                        _graphics    =    new
GraphicsDeviceManager(this);
        Content.RootDirectory = "Content";
        IsMouseVisible = true;
    }


    protected³ override void Initialize()
    {
            // Initialize⁴ game elements (paddles,
ball, etc.)
            _leftPaddlePosition = new Vector2(50,
200);
            _rightPaddlePosition = new Vector2(700,
200);
        _ballPosition = new Vector2(400, 200);
        _ballVelocity = new Vector2(2, 2);
        base.Initialize();
    }


    protected override void LoadContent()
    {
                            _spriteBatch    =    new
SpriteBatch(GraphicsDevice);
                            _paddleTexture    =
Content.Load<Texture2D>("paddle");⁵
                            _ballTexture    =
Content.Load<Texture2D>("ball");
    }


        protected    override    void    Update(GameTime
gameTime)
    {
                                                if⁶
(GamePad.GetState(PlayerIndex.One).Buttons.Back
```

```
==             ButtonState.Pressed              ||
Keyboard.GetState().IsKeyDown(Keys.Escape))
            Exit();

            // Update⁷ game state (move paddles,
ball, check collisions)
        UpdatePaddles();
        UpdateBall();
        base.Update(gameTime);
    }


    protected override void Draw(GameTime
gameTime)
    {

GraphicsDevice.Clear(Color.CornflowerBlue);

        _spriteBatch.Begin();⁸
        // Draw game elements (paddles, ball)
            _spriteBatch.Draw(_paddleTexture,
_leftPaddlePosition, Color.White);
            _spriteBatch.Draw(_paddleTexture,
_rightPaddlePosition, Color.White);
            _spriteBatch.Draw(_ballTexture,
_ballPosition, Color.White);
        _spriteBatch.End();⁹

        base.Draw(gameTime);
    }

    private void UpdatePaddles()
    {
        // Handle player input to move paddles
    }
```

```
    private void UpdateBall()
    {
        // Update ball position based on velocity
        // Check for collisions with paddles and
walls
    }
}
```

Explanation:

This code creates a basic MonoGame window.

`Initialize()` sets up the initial positions of the paddles and ball.

`LoadContent()` loads the textures for the paddles and ball.

`Update()` handles game logic, such as moving the paddles and ball and checking for collisions.

`Draw()` renders the game elements on the screen.

This is a simplified example to illustrate the basic structure. You'll need to implement the `UpdatePaddles()` and `UpdateBall()` methods to handle player input, ball movement, collision detection, scoring, and other game logic.

By building this simple Pong game, you'll gain hands-on experience with game development concepts and learn how to use C# and MonoGame to create 2D games. Remember to explore MonoGame's documentation and examples to learn more about its features and capabilities.

9.3 Exploring 3D Game Development Options with .NET

While 2D games have their charm, the world of 3D gaming offers incredible possibilities for immersive experiences and complex interactions. .NET has a growing presence in the 3D game development landscape, with powerful engines and frameworks that empower you to bring your 3D game ideas to life.

Why consider .NET for 3D game development?

C# familiarity: Leverage your existing C# skills and knowledge to develop gameplay logic, AI, and other game systems.

Performance: .NET's performance continues to improve, making it a viable option for demanding 3D games.

Cross-platform potential: Target multiple platforms, including Windows, macOS, Linux, and potentially consoles with the right engine.

Strong tooling: Visual Studio and Visual Studio Code provide excellent debugging and development support for C# and .NET.

Growing ecosystem: The .NET ecosystem for game development is expanding with new libraries, frameworks, and engines.

Popular 3D game engines and frameworks for .NET

Unity:

Industry standard: Unity is a dominant force in game development, widely used for both 2D and 3D games.

C# scripting: Unity uses C# as its primary scripting language, making it a natural choice for .NET developers.

Extensive features: Unity boasts a vast array of features, including a visual editor, physics engine, animation system, and a massive asset store.

Cross-platform support: Deploy your games to various platforms, including Windows, macOS, Linux, iOS, Android, and consoles.

Stride (formerly Xenko):

Open-source power: Stride is a powerful open-source game engine with a focus on 3D graphics and visual scripting.

C# foundation: Stride uses C# as its core language for scripting and game logic.

High-fidelity graphics: Stride excels at rendering stunning 3D graphics with advanced features like physically based rendering (PBR).

Active development: Stride is actively developed with a growing community and regular updates.

Wave Engine:

.NET-centric: Wave Engine is built entirely on .NET, providing a familiar environment for .NET developers.

Versatile: Suitable for both 2D and 3D game development.

Visual editor and scripting: Offers a visual editor and C# scripting for creating game logic and interactions.

Cross-platform reach: Deploy your games to Windows, macOS, Linux, iOS, Android, and other platforms.

CRYENGINE:

AAA powerhouse: CRYENGINE is a high-fidelity game engine known for its stunning graphics and realistic physics.

C# integration: CRYENGINE provides a C# framework for developing gameplay logic and interacting with the engine.

Advanced features: Offers advanced features like real-time ray tracing, volumetric fog, and realistic water simulations.

Choosing the right engine

Consider these factors when choosing a 3D game engine for your .NET project:

Project scope: Is it a small indie game or a large-scale project?

Graphics requirements: What level of visual fidelity are you aiming for?

Team skills: Does your team have experience with the engine or are you willing to learn?

Platform targets: Which platforms do you want to support?

Budget and licensing: Is the engine open-source, commercially licensed, or royalty-based?

Getting started with 3D game development in .NET

Choose an engine: Select a 3D game engine that aligns with your project goals and preferences.

Learn the engine: Familiarize yourself with the engine's features, tools, and workflow through tutorials and documentation.

Start with a simple project: Begin with a small, manageable project to gain experience with the engine and 3D game development concepts.

Join the community: Engage with the engine's community to seek help, share your work, and learn from others.

By exploring these 3D game development options with .NET, you can tap into a world of creative possibilities and build immersive and engaging 3D game experiences.

Chapter 10

The Future of C# and Cross-Platform Development

10.1 Emerging Trends and Technologies in the .NET Ecosystem

The .NET ecosystem is constantly evolving, with new trends and technologies emerging to empower developers and shape the future of software development. Here are some key trends to watch:

1. .NET 8 and Beyond:

Performance Enhancements: Each new .NET release brings performance improvements, making applications faster and more efficient. .NET 8 continues this trend with a focus on optimizing runtime performance and reducing memory consumption.

Unified Platform: .NET continues its journey towards a unified platform, making it easier to build applications across different domains (web, desktop, mobile, cloud, gaming, IoT).

Modernized Features: .NET is actively incorporating modern language features and paradigms, such as improved asynchronous programming, enhanced pattern matching, and better support for functional programming concepts.

2. Blazor and Full-Stack Web Development:

Blazor WebAssembly: Blazor enables building interactive web UIs with C# instead of JavaScript, running directly in the browser. This allows for full-stack web development with .NET, sharing code and skills between the front-end and back-end.

Blazor Server: Blazor Server provides another approach for building web UIs with C#, where the UI logic runs on the server and updates are sent to the client over a real-time connection.

Hybrid scenarios: Blazor can be used in hybrid scenarios, combining Blazor components with traditional JavaScript frameworks.

3. AI and Machine Learning with ML.NET:

ML.NET Integration: ML.NET is an open-source machine learning framework for .NET developers. It allows you to integrate machine learning models into your applications for tasks like classification, regression, clustering, and anomaly detection.

AI-powered applications: .NET is increasingly being used to build AI-powered applications, leveraging ML.NET and other AI services like Azure Cognitive Services.

4. Microservices and Cloud-Native Development:

Microservices Architecture: .NET is well-suited for building microservices architectures, with lightweight frameworks like ASP.NET Core and support for containerization technologies like Docker.

Cloud-Native Development: .NET is increasingly being used for cloud-native development, with excellent support for Azure services and cloud-native patterns.

5. Cross-Platform Development with .NET MAUI:

Modern UI Framework: .NET MAUI is the evolution of Xamarin.Forms, providing a modern and unified framework for building native UIs across mobile and desktop platforms.

Single Codebase: .NET MAUI allows you to write your UI and application logic once and deploy it to iOS, Android, Windows, and macOS.

6. DevOps and CI/CD:

DevOps Practices: .NET development is embracing DevOps practices, with tools and integrations for continuous integration, continuous delivery, and automated testing.

Azure DevOps: Azure DevOps provides a comprehensive set of tools for managing the entire software development lifecycle, from planning[1] and development to testing and deployment.

7. Low-Code and No-Code Platforms:

.NET Integration: Low-code and no-code platforms are becoming more popular, and .NET is integrating with these platforms to provide extensibility and customization options.

Power Platform: Microsoft's Power Platform, which includes Power Apps and Power Automate, allows users to build applications and automate workflows with minimal coding, often leveraging .NET for custom logic and integrations.

8. Focus on Security:

Secure Coding Practices: .NET continues to emphasize secure coding practices and provides tools and libraries to help developers build secure applications.

Security First Approach: Security is being integrated into every aspect of .NET development, from language features to development tools and cloud services.

9. Testing and Automation:

Testing Frameworks: .NET offers robust testing frameworks like xUnit, NUnit, and MSTest for unit testing, integration testing, and end-to-end testing.

Test Automation: Test automation is becoming increasingly important, with tools and frameworks for automating various testing tasks.

By staying informed about these emerging trends and technologies, .NET developers can leverage the latest advancements to build innovative, high-quality, and future-proof applications.

10.2 NET MAUI Evolution: Roadmap and Future Enhancements

.NET MAUI is a relatively young framework, but it's evolving rapidly with a promising roadmap and exciting enhancements on the horizon. Microsoft is actively investing in .NET MAUI to make it the premier framework for building cross-platform native applications.

Recent Enhancements (.NET 8)

Improved Performance: .NET 8 brought significant performance improvements to MAUI, resulting in faster startup times, smoother animations, and reduced memory consumption.

New Controls and Features: New controls like `Map` and `WebView` have been introduced, along with enhancements to existing controls and layouts.

Enhanced Platform Integration: Better integration with platform-specific APIs and features, enabling developers to access more native capabilities.

Tooling Improvements: Visual Studio and Visual Studio Code continue to receive updates with better support for .NET MAUI development, including improved debugging, hot reload, and IntelliSense.

Roadmap and Future Enhancements

While the exact roadmap is subject to change, here are some key areas of focus for future .NET MAUI development:

Performance Optimization: Continuous focus on improving performance across all platforms, including startup time, rendering speed, and memory usage.

New Controls and Features: Expanding the set of built-in controls and features to cover more use cases and provide richer UI capabilities.

Enhanced Platform Integration: Deeper integration with platform-specific APIs and features, allowing developers to leverage the unique capabilities of each platform.

Improved Developer Experience: Streamlining the development process with better tooling, enhanced debugging, and improved hot reload capabilities.

Community Engagement: Active engagement with the .NET MAUI community to gather feedback, address issues, and incorporate community contributions.

Desktop Enhancements: Further improvements for desktop development, including better support for windowing, menus, and platform-specific desktop features.

3D Graphics Support: Exploring possibilities for 3D graphics rendering within .NET MAUI, potentially leveraging technologies like OpenGL or Vulkan.

AR/VR Integration: Investigating integration with augmented reality (AR) and virtual reality (VR) platforms and SDKs.

Key Areas of Innovation

Blazor Hybrid: Combining Blazor with .NET MAUI to build hybrid applications that blend web and native UI components. This allows developers to leverage web technologies while still accessing native device features.

.NET MAUI with Blazor: Using Blazor components directly within .NET MAUI applications to build interactive UIs with C# instead of relying on traditional XAML.

Modernized Architecture: Continuously evolving the architecture of .NET MAUI to leverage the latest advancements in .NET and provide a more modular and extensible framework.

Staying Informed

To stay informed about the latest .NET MAUI developments, refer to these resources:

.NET MAUI Blog: https://devblogs.microsoft.com/dotnet/

.NET MAUI GitHub Repository: https://github.com/dotnet/maui

.NET   MAUI   Documentation: https://learn.microsoft.com/en-us/dotnet/maui/

By keeping an eye on the .NET MAUI roadmap and future enhancements, you can stay ahead of the curve and leverage the latest advancements to build cutting-edge cross-platform applications.

10.3 Building Modern, Scalable, and Future-Proof Applications with C#

The software development landscape is constantly changing, with new technologies and trends emerging at a rapid pace. To build applications that stand the test of time, it's essential to adopt a forward-thinking approach and leverage the tools and techniques that promote scalability, maintainability, and adaptability. C# and the .NET ecosystem provide a strong foundation for building modern, scalable, and future-proof applications.

Key Principles

Embrace Cloud-Native Development:

Microservices: Decompose your application into smaller, independent microservices that can be developed, deployed, and scaled independently.

Containers: Utilize containerization technologies like Docker to package your applications and their dependencies for consistent deployment across different environments.

Serverless: Leverage serverless computing platforms like Azure Functions to run event-driven code without managing infrastructure.

Cloud Services: Integrate with cloud services like Azure Storage, Azure Cosmos DB, and Azure AI to enhance your application's capabilities.

Design for Scalability:

Horizontal Scaling: Architect your application to scale horizontally by adding more instances to handle increased load.

Asynchronous Programming: Utilize asynchronous programming techniques (`async` and `await`) to improve responsiveness and efficiency.

Caching: Implement caching strategies to reduce redundant data access and improve performance.

Load Balancing: Distribute traffic across multiple instances to prevent overload and ensure high availability.

Prioritize Maintainability:

Clean Code: Write clean, well-structured code that is easy to understand and maintain.

SOLID Principles: Follow SOLID principles (Single Responsibility, Open/Closed, Liskov Substitution, Interface Segregation, Dependency Inversion) to create[1] modular and maintainable code.

Design Patterns: Utilize design patterns to solve common problems and improve code organization.

Code Reviews: Conduct regular code reviews to ensure code quality and consistency.

Ensure Adaptability:

Loose Coupling: Design components with loose coupling to minimize dependencies and facilitate changes.

Modular Design: Break down your application into modular components that can be easily replaced or updated.

API-First Approach: Design APIs that are well-defined, versioned, and documented to enable integration with other systems.

Embrace Change: Be prepared to adapt to new technologies and trends as they emerge.

Focus on Security:

Security by Design: Integrate security considerations into every stage of the development process.

Authentication and Authorization: Implement strong authentication and authorization mechanisms to protect user data and resources.

Data Protection: Encrypt sensitive data, validate user input, and follow secure coding practices to prevent vulnerabilities.

Security Auditing: Conduct regular security audits and penetration testing to identify and address weaknesses.

Leverage the .NET Ecosystem:

.NET MAUI: Build cross-platform native UIs for mobile and desktop with .NET MAUI.

Blazor: Develop interactive web UIs with C# using Blazor.

ML.NET: Integrate machine learning models into your applications with ML.NET.

Azure Services: Utilize Azure services to enhance your application's capabilities and scalability.

By adhering to these principles and leveraging the power of C# and the .NET ecosystem, you can build modern, scalable, and future-proof applications that meet the evolving needs of your users and business.